CW00497513

Original Title: Shattered Mirrors

Editors: Theodor Taimla
Autor: Melani Helimets
ISBN: 978-9916-748-86-2

Shattered Mirrors

Melani Helimets

Shattered Light Symphony

In skies where whispers softly blend,
A symphony of light does fade.
Broken prisms twist and bend,
Casting shadows, hues displayed.

Through cracks in time, the silence falls,
Each note a fragment of the past.
Echoes chase through empty halls,
Their melodies too bright to last.

Reflections dance on mirrored waves,
While stars above shed tears of gold.
In twilight's grasp, the night enslaves,
The shattered light, a tale retold.

Fragmented Realities

In dreams where waking thoughts collide,
A thousand worlds are torn apart.
Each fragment holds what we confide,
Of endless realms within the heart.

Through mists of doubt, the past does turn,
To faces lost in shadowed haze.
Memories in fragments burn,
As time consumes those fleeting days.

The echoes of what once might be,
Now linger in a fractured veil.
Beyond, the silent sea,
Where broken truths and lies prevail.

Splintered Truths

In every word, a hidden scar,
Splintered truths that twist the tale.
Beneath the surface, never far,
Lies the thread that we unveil.

Each secret wears a fragile mask,
In whispered breaths, deceit concealed.
Seeking answers in our task,
Through splintered truths, the heart revealed.

In shards of glass, reflections wane,
Lost in fragments, we remain.
Yet through the echoes of our pain,
A splintered truth begins again.

Fragmented Echoes

In the chamber of forgotten dreams,
A whisper lingers, softly beams.
Fragments scatter, shards of light,
Echoes dance, through endless night.

Silent shadows shift and sway,
Hopes once bright, now lost, astray.
A memory calls from distant past,
Fading echoes, will they last?

Ghosts of joy, and spectral tears,
Mingle in the twilight years.
Shattered moments, left behind,
Fragmented echoes, intertwined.

Splinters in the Soul

Hidden scars beneath the skin,
Splinters from where dreams begin.
Silent cries that no one hears,
Wounded by unspoken fears.

Pieces lost in time's embrace,
Mark the soul with quiet grace.
Fragmented bits of joy and pain,
Whisper truths in sorrow's reign.

Unknown paths, and silent screams,
Haunt the nights and taint the dreams.
Splinters deep within the soul,
Seeking light to make them whole.

Dispersed Light

Glimmers fade in twilight's breath,
Scattered light defies its death.
Through the veil, a fractured beam,
Shining forth in dreamlike gleam.

Fragments of a broken star,
Spread their light both near and far.
Weave a tapestry of night,
Dispersed whispers, sweet delight.

In the chaos of the dark,
Tiny flares ignite a spark.
Dispersed light in shadow's grip,
Guides the heart on its lone trip.

Broken Brilliance

Once a flame that burned so bright,
Now lies shattered in the night.
Fragments of a fiery soul,
Scattered dreams take their toll.

In the dark, a spark remains,
Brilliance lost through silent pains.
Pieces glisten, stars reborn,
From the night, new dawn is torn.

Broken brilliance, in the sky,
Shines anew, as shadows die.
Through the night and into day,
Shattered light will find its way.

The Shard Parade

In the twilight's gentle fade,
March the shards, a fine cascade.
Reflections of the day's charade,
In the eve, their dance portrayed.

Mirror fragments, tempest's braid,
Glittering steps in night's arcade.
Ghosts of light in dark invade,
Through the ether they parade.

Whispers carried, secrets weighed,
In their silence, truth conveyed.
Spectral notes, a serenade,
In the wind, their form displayed.

Fragmented Hall of Echoes

In halls where shadows, echoes fall,
Fragments speak in muffled call.
Whispers trace the sultry wall,
Answering the silent thrall.

Voices of the past entwine,
Memories both dark, divine.
Each word an echo, clear as wine,
Splintered thoughts in labyrinths align.

Silent steps on time's foreboding,
Each an echo dimly floating.
Memories, an endless voting,
Fragment tales in halls, parading.

Disintegrating Glances

Eyes that meet in fleeting trance,
Seconds pass in wordless dance.
Moments fade, a fractal chance,
Disintegrating at a glance.

Gazes held in silent fervor,
Every look a fragile server.
Worlds within, they softly shiver,
Disappearing down the river.

Each encounter, worlds collide,
In their depths, we briefly hide.
Ephemeral as the shifting tide,
Disintegrate in glances, wide.

Splintered Universes

Night unfolds as stars collide,
Splintered beams in void abide.
Worlds within each ray confide,
Secrets of the astral tide.

Galaxies in fractured rifts,
Cosmic shards, the ether sifts.
Each a universe adrift,
Spanning aeons, moving swift.

Nebulas in pieces shorn,
Night's illusion, worlds reborn.
In the splinters, life is sworn,
Universes torn and worn.

Fractured Glimpses

In twilight's shadow, whispers grow,
Among the stars, where breezes blow,
Fragments dance in night's embrace,
Echoes lost, but never replaced.

Dreams in shards, a scattered light,
Memories flicker, out of sight,
Time's mosaic, pieces stray,
Silent secrets on display.

All that's fractured, beauty in flaws,
Silent whispers, time's applause,
Moments slip through fingers fast,
Glimpses of a fractured past.

Threads of stories, woven tight,
Day turns to an endless night,
In the cracks, the world reveals,
Fractured glimpses, truth conceals.

Ephemeral, these shards of time,
Songs unsung, without a rhyme,
In the darkness, light persists,
Fractured glimpses, life insists.

Shards of Memory Lane

Down the path where echoes lay,
Silent whispers guide the way,
Shards of past, in subtle glow,
Trace the steps we've come to know.

Every fragment tells a tale,
A fleeting ship without a sail,
Moments frozen, time refrains,
Pieces of forgotten rains.

Faded laughter, distant cries,
Starlit nights and bright blue skies,
Memories in pieces strewn,
Golden dusk and silvery moon.

Through the haze, the past returns,
In the heart, a fire burns,
Shards connect the long-lost days,
Woven in the twilight's haze.

Lost and found, we wander still,
Down the lane, with empty fill,
In each shard, a life concealed,
Memories in light revealed.

Mirrored Disputes

In the glass, reflections lie,
Mirror's depth, a silent sigh,
Faces fracture, thoughts entwine,
Mirrored souls, a fractured line.

Arguments in silent streams,
Mirror holds our deepest dreams,
Words unspoken, tensions flare,
Mirrored disputes, laid bare.

Eyes that question, hearts that dart,
In the mirror, shadows start,
Silent echoes, battles fought,
Disputes in reflections caught.

Reality in shards of glass,
Truths and lies that come to pass,
Mirrored disputes, quiet rage,
In the glass, a fractured stage.

Endless cycle, back and forth,
North to south, and south to north,
In reflections, hope and pain,
Mirrored disputes, love's refrain.

Broken Glimpses

Shattered dusk in twilight's hands,
Broken glimpses, fleeting strands,
Moments lost, yet somehow near,
Fragments of a yesteryear.

Whispered sighs and silent calls,
Pieces hidden, outer walls,
Light through cracks, where shadows gleam,
Glimpses of a fractured dream.

In the void, the echoes play,
Through the mist, the memories stay,
Broken paths where stories weave,
Time's illusion, we believe.

In the fissures, life shines bright,
Shattered moments, pure delight,
Broken glimpses, shade, and light,
Day transitions into night.

Hands reach out to touch the past,
Broken glimpses hold us fast,
In each shard, a world unfolds,
Tales of silver, streaks of gold.

Fractured Beams

In twilight's cold embrace
Soft shadows weave a tale
Of fractured beams and dreams
Where whispered winds prevail

Splintered light cascades
Through cracks in ancient time
Revealing hidden paths
Where silent spirits climb

The golden dusk departs
Replaced by silver nights
In fractured beams they dance
With waltzing spectral lights

Echoes of the past
Reside in beams once whole
Fragmented, etched in fate
The wraiths that time console

In every shattered ray
A story comes alive
Fractured beams align
Where endless souls revive

Raptured Reflections

Beneath the dusky sky
The mirror holds its truth
In raptured reflections drawn
Of age and fleeting youth

Glimmers of the past
Adorn the water's face
Raptured reflections speak
In somber, silent grace

Ripples kiss the light
Distorting visions clear
In raptured reflections, hues
Of love and softened fear

Crystal pools reveal
The tales of yesteryear
Raptured in a gaze
Their secrets, ever near

In every mirrored glance
A universe unfolds
Raptured reflections bind
The stories seldom told

Splintered Musings

In the quiet of the night
Splintered musings rise
Thoughts that fracture calmly
Beneath the starry skies

Fragments of the mind
Scatter in the dark
Splintered musings whisper
Leaving just a spark

Each shard of dream and notion
Floats within the air
Splintered musings silently
Invite the heart to dare

Memories split and scatter
Pieces of a whole
Splintered musings echo
Through the depth of soul

In every broken fragment
A world both lost and found
Splintered musings weave
Where endless thoughts are bound

Ghosts of the Pane

Against the window's frame
Press shadows of the past
Ghosts of the pane cast figures
In moonlight's gentle grasp

Silent specters hide
Within the glassy sheen
Ghosts of the pane emerge
In spectral silvered gleam

Reflections of the lost
In panes both old and worn
Ghosts of the pane ensnare
The souls in nighttime born

Each flicker holds a tale
Of those who walked before
Ghosts of the pane reveal
The dreams of timeless lore

In every glassy shard
Their presence we attain
Ghosts of the pane remain
Beyond the mortal plain

Pieces of the Self

Fragments of memory, scattered in the breeze
Threads of identity, caught in life's tease
Moments of laughter, interwoven with fears
Tapestry of existence, woven through years

Reflections in mirrors, ever shifting frames
Silent whispers echo, calling out names
Shards of the past, glimmer in the night
Emerging softly, in the pale moonlight

Emotion's mosaic, colors bold and bright
Tears and joys merge, in the prism of sight
Pieces of the self, a puzzle to decipher
In the heart's chamber, the soul grows wiser

Broken Glass Dreams

Shattered aspirations, like glass on the floor
Dreams once whole, now a chaotic encore
Hopes turned to shrapnel, glisten in the sun
Pieces of possibility, lost one by one

Reflections on pavements, fragment in the light
Spectacles of sorrow, in the quiet night
Fragile illusions, break with a sigh
Scattered ambitions, in the blink of an eye

From the ruins, new visions arise
Gardens of tomorrow, in unexpected guise
Gather the fragments, and gently mend
Create a future, where dreams transcend

Echoes of Silver Slivers

In the stillness, whispers of the past
Silver slivers gleam, in shadows cast
Echoes of moments, soft as morning dew
Stories of time, retold anew

Fragments of laughter, drift on the air
Ghosts of smiles, lingering in despair
Glimmers of hope, in the twilight's glow
In the silent night, memories flow

Waves of reflection, wash on the shore
Silver slivers shimmer, evermore
Echoes carry, a tale untold
In the heart's silence, they find their hold

Splintered Realities

Parallel worlds, drifting apart
Splintered realities, an intricate art
Fragments of truth, scattered like leaves
Shifting dimensions, no one believes

Mirrors of existence, crack and reform
Seen through a prism, a multiverse born
Flickering images, dance through the night
Fading in shadows, igniting in light

Chasing illusions, through corridors vast
Piecing together the future from the past
In the kaleidoscope, visions collide
In splintered realities, worlds coincide

Scattered Images

In the mind's vast gallery, visions float
Across the canvases of thought and dream,
They twirl in colors, bright they gloat,
Yet fade away like morning's beam.

Moments flash and fade to gray,
Echoes of a time once whole,
Glimpses of what may or may,
Be fragments that complete the soul.

Memories stutter then dissolve,
Into a murmured, silent hum,
As phantom faces turn and evolve,
In the theater of the inscrutable numb.

Seeking shapes in scattered light,
To piece together what was fraught,
In the kaleidoscope of night,
Where scattered images are caught.

Broken Lens

A shattered glimpse of what remains,
Through glass that cracked and split,
Reflections twisted by the pains,
Of truths we hesitate to admit.

In distorted worlds we gaze in awe,
Through prisms carved from loss,
Each shard reveals an unseen flaw,
That bridges chasms we can't cross.

Visions blur and clarity eludes,
Where light refracts and breaks,
In a spectrum of muted hues,
The heart in tender ache partakes.

Mirrors fragmented, mirrored scenes,
Echoes half of what they've been,
Through the landscape of shattered dreams,
We trace the fractures time has seen.

Fragile Perceptions

Thoughts fragile in their scaffolding,
Precarious towers of what's perceived,
Each delicate layer mildly trembling,
In the breeze of doubt believed.

Ideas like glass, so clear yet frail,
In moments of clarity so rare,
They glisten softly then grow pale,
Lost in the tenuous air.

Emotions drape their silken veil,
Over the fabric of our mind,
Yet at a whisper's touch may fail,
Leaving disquieting voids behind.

Perceptions teeter on the brink,
Of shattering in the storm of fear,
In each fleeting thought we sink,
Hoping truth may still appear.

Shards of Light

In the darkness slivers pierce,
Shards of light that fight to hold,
Through the blackened night they pierce,
A mosaic story softly told.

Fragments float in the abyss,
Glimmering whispers of the day,
As shadows dance in silent bliss,
In a fleeting, fragile array.

Cracks allow the beams to seep,
Where night and light converge,
Ephemeral in their luminous leap,
A transient, glowing surge.

In the tapestry of endless night,
Each shard a story juxtaposed,
We gather dreams in pieces tight,
In the symphony of light composed.

Shattered Hues

Colors of the dusk, once a vivid spree,
Now lie fractured, like leaves in the breeze.
Whispers of twilight, shadows softly skew,
A dance of nightfall in shattered hues.

Echoes of morning, shards of fragile light,
Splinters of dawn in a battle's quiet.
Fragments of yesterday, scattered and used,
Pastel dreams in a canvas abused.

Enigmatic silence, whispers in the dew,
Morning paints the horizon anew.
But the cracks remain, like invisible clues,
In the tapestry of shattered hues.

Fragmented Glow

Behind the veil of a broken smile,
Lies the semblance of serenity's wile.
A heart in fragments, pure as snow,
Glimmers faintly—a fragmented glow.

In the twilight's embrace, under starry dome,
Dreams linger softly, like waves of foam.
Amidst the darkness, their radiance flows,
Carving paths in a fragmented glow.

In mirrors shattered, reflections sigh,
Pieces remain of a radiant sky.
Twinkling remnants, in the night's tableau,
Illuminate the shadows—a fragmented glow.

Crushed Reflections

Beyond the river, where mirrors lie,
Crushed reflections beneath the sky.
Silent ripples in the moon's caress,
Capture moments of broken finesse.

The wind whispers secrets of days gone by,
While reflections wane and slowly die.
In every fragment, echoes of affection,
Life's dichotomy in crushed reflection.

Moonlight dances on a solemn stream,
Awakens memories like a distant dream.
Shattered by time, in mild recollections,
Ever lost in the crushed reflections.

Glass Wounds

In the silence of a moonlit night,
Where shadows dance and dreams take flight.
Glass wounds whisper tales untold,
Of hearts that shattered, of love grown cold.

Through the veil of sorrow's deep embrace,
Memories linger in a fragile place.
Every shard a scar, a truth revealed,
In glass wounds, time remains unhealed.

Beneath the starlight, in whispers found,
Pain and beauty in a haunting sound.
In every fragment, a story looms,
Etched in the depths of glass wounds.

Splintered Hues

In a prism of splintered hues,

the colors intertwine,
as life unfurls its canvas,
in shades both dim and fine.

Each fragment tells a tale,
of joy, of pain, of dreams,
pieced together in a mosaic,
where nothing's as it seems.

We find beauty in the broken,
in every fractured part,
for splintered hues combine,
to paint the human heart.

Broken Whispers

In broken whispers of the night,
the secrets softly flow,
like echoes in a canyon,
where shadows gently glow.

The murmurs wrap around us,
concealing truths untold,
we strain to catch their meaning,
before the dawn unfolds.

Each whisper holds a story,
of love, of loss, of fears,
a tapestry of silence,
woven through the years.

Distorted Glances

Through lenses cracked and shaded,

distorted glances fall,
reality is twisted,
not recognizable at all.

What mirrors show is fleeting,
a fragment of the whole,
distorted visions mingle,
with the contours of our soul.

In the kaleidoscope of life,
where clarity oft fades,
we find the truth in pieces,
amidst the shifting shades.

Cracked Surfaces

In the silence, whispers break,
Songs of things we can't remake.
Lines and fissures, time's own trace,
On our hearts, we find a place.

Shadows dance on broken stone,
Echoes of what's overthrown.
Mosaic dreams, a fractured call,
Pieces long to be made whole.

Reflections in each shattered shard,
Memories held, silently scarred.
Beauty found in imperfection,
Life's own tender resurrection.

Nature laughs at human flaw,
Cracks are where it writes its law.
Growth from what's been torn apart,
Healing in the hardened heart.

In the end, we stand and see,
Courage in this broken sea.
Cracks that show life's tender threads,
Love remains as fear but sheds.

Prism of Disarray

Colors twist and shadows bend,
Light refracts where endings blend.
In confusion, patterns sway,
Life turns in a grand ballet.

Harmony in chaos found,
Souls in disarray unbound.
Across the prism, light will stray,
Truths emerge in disarray.

Through the storm, a glimmer seen,
Madness births a calm serene.
In the broken, countless ways,
Paths converge in white and grays.

Chaos hums a wondrous tune,
Beneath the sun, beneath the moon.
Each disordered spectrum's play,
Dances in the light of day.

Though the world seems torn apart,
Prisms show creation's art.
In the scatter, beauty stays,
Finding peace in disarray.

Changelog of Self

Version notes on paper thin,
Scars of where we've each been in.
Updates penned in moments brief,
Coding life through joy and grief.

Beta dreams and alpha fears,
Patches over countless years.
Each release, a step refined,
Chasing wisdom close behind.

Lines of code that shape our fate,
Segfaults that we can't abate.
Pull requests to change our way,
Merge them in, without delay.

Documentation of the soul,
Logging each and every goal.
In each commit, a piece stored fast,
Lines reformed from memories past.

In this changelog, truth we find,
Echoes of a brilliant mind.
Self in progress, ever bright,
Coding patterns into light.

Glass Storm Torment

Through the tempest, shards do fly,
Cutting winds beneath the sky.
Glass in torment, shadows chase,
Waves of chaos in their place.

Fragile hearts in fury's grip,
Shattered dreams on each tight lip.
Storm within and storm outside,
In the glass, there's nowhere to hide.

Rains of sorrow, shards of pain,
Echoes of the lost refrain.
Whispers carried on the gale,
Hope, it sinks, and tempers wail.

Amidst the glass and storm's own cry,
Strength emerges, learns to fly.
From the shards, a light is born,
Rise anew from night to morn.

When the storm has passed us by,
Brilliant shards reflect the sky.
Torment's glass now turned to art,
Peace reclaimed within the heart.

Splintering Light

Through prisms the sun does break
Colors scatter, dreams awake
Luminous trails in the sky
Map a path where shadows lie

Cracks in dawn's cerulean glow
Reveal where hidden secrets flow
Splintering light, untamed and wild
Plays on the heart of a waking child

Mirrored lakes where beams refract
Show visions that the mind retracts
Waves of gold and sapphire gleam
Whisper tales of the unseen

Each shard a story, brightly sewn
In the canvas of the known
Splintering light, weave anew
Hope and wonder in your view

Dismantled Views

Fractured bridges, glassy strands
Dismantling borders, uncharted lands
Through scattered thoughts, pathways wind
In the fragments, truths we find

Broken frames of yesteryear
Pieces clear, though vision smeared
Reflect on pathways seldom walked
Where silent voices softly talked

Panoramas, once so whole
Disband to tell a richer scroll
In dismantled views, layers deep
Lie the treasures we still keep

Through shattered sights, understand
The beauty wrought by time's own hand
Dismantled views, past the fray
Guide us towards a clearer day

Broken Revelations

Shattered mirror, unearth sins
At edges, the truth begins
Revelations splinter, break
Life's pieces, a mosaic make

Secrets cast in silence, torn
Night's veil lifts at breaking morn
In every shard, a whispered tale
Of love, and loss, and steps so frail

From broken glass, a spectrum shines
Revealing woven, hidden lines
Each slight fragment, brightly bold
Carries stories untold

Through broken revelations, rise
New dawns under the fractured skies
In the fragments, wisdom find
The glue of heart and mind

Fragments of Reflection

In the mirror, fragments dance
Reflections caught by happenstance
Each piece, a world to explore
Timeless echoes from the core

Broken bits of yesteryears
Held along the path of tears
Reflection shows in parts and whole
The silent whispers of the soul

Fragments gleam as stars in night
Guiding thoughts in tenuous flight
In splinters found, a clearer view
Of life's paintings, brave and true

Through every minor fracture, see
The depth of self in clarity
Fragments of reflection, mend
Pathways where our hopes extend

Fractured Pane

A window sits with stories told,
Its glass now marred by time's harsh hand.
Through cracks, the sun's soft rays unfold,
Fragmented light in patterns grand.

Once clear and bright, the view it framed,
Now splintered shards paint twilight hues.
Whispering secrets, softly named,
Of dreams pursued and journeys new.

The world outside, a distant tale,
Distorted by the fractured view.
Life changes course like a ship's sail,
Unraveling truths we never knew.

Splintered Shadows

Beneath the moon's uncertain light,
Shadows dance, breaking apart.
Figures flicker in the night,
Echoes of a fractured heart.

Lost in paths of darkened woe,
Splintered shades of night unfold.
Faint whispers of the past bestow,
Secrets feared, yet stories bold.

In silence, shadows twist and lean,
Ghosts of memories once clear.
A dance of phantoms, so unseen,
Binding all that we hold dear.

Fragmented Memories

Through the mind's fragmented maze,
Echoes of the past remain.
Moments lost in time's long gaze,
Whispers of both joy and pain.

Snapshots hidden deep within,
Pieces of a broken past.
Each shard speaks of where we've been,
Memories that slowly last.

In the heart, these fragments lie,
Fragments of a life once whole.
As time's river passes by,
Binding story to the soul.

Crystalline Chaos

In the realm of shattered dreams,
Chaos blooms in crystal forms.
Patterns swirling in moonbeams,
Shapes defying all known norms.

Pieces scatter, breaking free,
Amidst the cosmos' endless dance.
Bound by neither land nor sea,
Lost in chaos, given chance.

Beauty in what's torn apart,
A disarray of fragile grace.
Fragmented art, from the heart,
A mirrored world in time and space.

Pieces of Self

In shards of glass, I see my face,
A puzzle scattered, out of place,
Fragments whisper, secrets sound,
Echoes lost, yet dreams unbound.

Thoughts like rivers, twist and wind,
Glimmers of a heart confined,
Hoping each small piece to find,
Wholeness unfelt, undefined.

Light through windows, broken rays,
Memories in vibrant sways,
Assembling moments, days and years,
Reconstructing joys and fears.

Hands collect, the fragments tender,
Piecing back what time may render,
In this mosaic, I discern,
The self rebuilt, to gently yearn.

Hope through cracks, a healing balm,
Whispers growing strong and calm,
Piece by piece, a soul refined,
Beauty in the fractured mined.

Fractured Facade

Behind the mask, a shadow's dance,
Stories told with every glance,
Cracks reveal a deeper view,
Truths unfolding, showing through.

A smile hides the weary heart,
In perfect roles, we play our part,
Yet whispers of a complete tale,
Through the fractures softly sail.

Eyes that hold a hidden beam,
Beyond the surface, deeper stream,
In the splinters, glimpses find,
The soul beyond the daily grind.

Mirrors shatter, faces clear,
Expressions raw, and thoughts sincere,
In the pieces, we discern,
The raw essence, we return.

Rebuilding from the shards of old,
Truth unmasked, a story told,
Fractured skin with tender care,
Revealing love beyond compare.

Torn Reflections

In reflections, torn and frayed,
I find the life that's been delayed,
Pieces scattered, here and there,
Echoes soft of memories fair.

Eyes against the mirror's gleam,
Past and present, merging seam,
In the rivers of the past,
Stories whispered, shadows cast.

Torn in thoughts, a mirrored state,
Memories that circulate,
Each reflection, light and dark,
Gives the soul its lasting mark.

Fragments of the time-worn glass,
Moments lived and moments pass,
In the pieces, dreams restore,
Whispers of what lies in store.

Kintsugi lines of gold entwine,
Torn reflections realign,
Beauty found in each repair,
Stories told with utmost care.

Splintered Prism

Splintered prism casts its light,
Scattering hues in darkest night,
Tiny shards and fragments glint,
Hope in broken beams of tint.

Colors dance on surfaces bare,
In each splinter, heart's soft flare,
Threads of light through shadows weave,
Tales of sorrow, webs of believe.

Prism's splinters, seeking whole,
Finding harmony in soul,
In the fractured light, we see,
Hidden depths of mystery.

Rainbows in the fragments blend,
Promises that never end,
Each a ray of what's to come,
Unity within the sum.

Splintered beauty, still it gleams,
Held together by our dreams,
In the prism's dance refrained,
Wholeness in the light retained.

Splinters in the Void

In the silence of the night,
Stars whisper, soft and bright.
Shards of dreams, sharp and cold,
Splinters in the void unfold.

Whispers carried by the breeze,
Secrets falling through the trees.
Fragments of a shattered mind,
Leaving broken hopes behind.

Cosmic dust ignites the sky,
Galaxies silently cry.
Through the darkness, sparks of light,
Splinters in infinite flight.

Endless echoes, void profound,
Lost souls in the silence drowned.
Celestial fractures, stories told,
In the void, dreams unrolled.

Nebulae's embrace, tender hues,
Colors mingling, myriad cues.
In the vast expanse, asteroids,
Falling splinters, fate avoids.

Scattered Echoes

Voices lost within the fold,
Whispers ancient, stories old.
Scattered echoes through the air,
Lingering dreams of those who dare.

Choruses of forgotten time,
Dissonant notes, untouched rhyme.
Memories in twilight hue,
Scattered echoes, old but new.

Through the valley, winds are calling,
Lost refrains in moonlight falling.
Each a note in cosmic play,
Scattered echoes, night and day.

Wanderers on paths untread,
Questions of the heart unsaid.
In the silence, they reside,
Scattered echoes, far and wide.

Silent murmurs of the past,
Moments fleeting, shadows cast.
In the ether, secrets flow,
Scattered echoes, ebb and glow.

Divided Lights

Glimmers in the breaking dawn,
Night and day in silent yawn.
Colors parting, skies ignite,
Divided lights, morning sight.

Radiance from a fractured source,
Twilight takes its destined course.
Splitting moments, shadows fade,
Divided lights, a solemn trade.

Stars retreat to spectral sleep,
While the sun its vigils keep.
Where they meet on horizon's edge,
Divided lights in solemn pledge.

Whispers of the coming night,
Sundown's glow, a waning light.
Balancing on beams of gold,
Divided lights, stories told.

In the dark, the moon ascends,
Lonely beams as night pretends.
United through celestial fight,
Divided lights, a timeless sight.

Dissonant Reflections

Mirrors of a fractured soul,
Seeking ways to become whole.
In the glass, they twist and bend,
Dissonant reflections mend.

Through the prism's complex hues,
Truths and lies both subtly fuse.
Fragmented self in silent dance,
Dissonant reflections chance.

Light and shadow intertwine,
Secrets hidden in the shine.
In the depths, a story lies,
Dissonant reflections rise.

Cosmic forces on the seam,
Reality, a waking dream.
Through the lens of time and space,
Dissonant reflections trace.

Ephemeral the moments drift,
Shifting views and thoughts adrift.
In each surface, lives a face,
Dissonant reflections grace.

Echoes of Glass

Whispers in the night breeze
Glimmers fade from sight
Shattered pieces tell
Stories etched in light

Dreams once whole and clear
Now a jagged mass
Reflections dance, disperse
On the floor of glass

Echoes of a time long past
Haunt the empty hall
Every footstep resonates
With the crystal's call

Fragments catching moonlight
Spark a fleeting glow
Memories in shards of glass
Through the depths they flow

In the silent aftermath
Goes the fragile sound
Of echoes gently fading
Where broken dreams are found

Smashed Realities

In a world gone awry
Mirrors can't hold true
Every image splintered
Leaves a skewed view

Hopes once cast in silver
Now a pale debris
Scattered reflections mar
Our blurred reality

Visions of what may be
Lie in ruined seas
A kaleidoscope of dreams
Broken by the breeze

Each shattered moment speaks
Of what could have been
Pieces of existence
Lie bare to be seen

From these ruins, a tale
Of love and of loss
Smashed realities holding
All we dare emboss

Fragmenting Light

Sunrise meets the twilight
With a fractured beam
Through the prisms of time
Shards of thought do gleam

Colors blend and scatter
In a mist of white
Every ray dissects fate
Fragmenting the light

A prism's every facet
Holds a world confined
In each split of brilliance
Past and future bind

Rainbows born of sorrow
Paint the ethers wide
Fragmenting light shows tears
That the stars can't hide

Refractions of a moment
Across the void span
Light's eternal fracture
In the palm of man

Brittle Visions

In the haze of morning
Dreams begin to fade
Images once vivid
Now a dull parade

Brittle visions shatter
Under glance's weight
Flimsy as the sunshine
Touching on the gate

Memories like paper
Fold and crease with time
Past the brittle visions
Climbing life's tall climb

Delicate as whispers
From a bygone land
Visions break with the dawn
In the heart's own hand

In a world so fragile
Why do we pretend
Brittle visions, echo
Till the daylight's end

Splinters of the Soul

In shadows cast by twilight's veil,
Whispers of what once was whole,
A fractured heart begins to pale,
Splinters drifting from the soul.

Through silent nights and restless dreams,
Pieces scatter, lost in time,
Echoes of forgotten schemes,
Reside in fragments, left behind.

Yet from the shards, new light will glow,
Mosaic formed of love and pain,
In every fracture, strength will grow,
A phoenix rising once again.

So let the splinters weave their art,
A tapestry of broken grace,
Healing starts within the heart,
A mended soul finds its place.

Embrace the journey, scars and all,
For every piece a story tells,
From scattered fragments, stand tall,
As the silent night dispels.

Through the Broken Pane

Through the broken pane, a world askew,
Visions dancing in the light,
Diamond edges, morning dew,
Silent whispers of the night.

Shattered fragments, prisms bright,
Catch the dawn with fractured gleam,
Hope rekindled, pure despite,
Midnight's melancholy dream.

Reflections twist, distorted true,
Mirror realms of shadowed past,
Fragments framing what's in view,
Holding moments meant to last.

Yet in the cracks, new worlds arise,
Stories hidden in the seams,
Broken panes become the eyes,
Through which the soul redeems.

Puzzle pieces, scattered wide,
Forming something wholly new,
In each shard, a truth implied,
Beyond the broken glass, a view.

Crystallized Chaos

Chaos spins in crystal light,
Prisms fracture, shapes undone,
Order lost in endless night,
Patterns break where dreams begun.

Glimmered shards of what could be,
Dance within the storm's embrace,
Formless moments, wild and free,
Through the chaos, find their place.

Each fragment, a design unique,
In the swirl of time and space,
Nature's whim in havoc's streak,
Art emerges, raw with grace.

From the tempest, calm will rise,
Crystallized through storm's decay,
Beauty forms before our eyes,
Clarity in disarray.

Embrace the chaos, crystal hue,
Find the art within the storm,
Life in shards appears anew,
Chaos will its shape transform.

Ruins of Reflection

In ruins of reflection's past,
Ghostly echoes whisper low,
Memories in shadows cast,
Where the silent waters flow.

Forgotten walls and weathered stone,
Hold the tales of yesteryears,
Silent voices, all alone,
Speak of joy, and speak of tears.

In the stillness, time stands still,
Echoes weave a tapestry,
Of broken dreams and iron will,
In the ruins, find the key.

For in the cracks of walls once strong,
New growth emerges through the strife,
Echoes merge into a song,
Resurrecting former life.

So in the ruins, do not fear,
Reflections guide a journey new,
Stories waiting, crystal clear,
In ancient halls, the light shines through.

Frayed Reflections

In mirrors, lies the tangled glass,
Where echoes from the past will pass,
A heart's distortions, shadows cast,
Through fog and mist they travel fast.

Whispers born of fractured light,
Days wrapped in endless twilight,
Memories wane with the falling night,
Dreams dissolve from sightless height.

Navigating paths once tread,
Ghostly figures softly tread,
Through rivers flowing in the head,
Silent conversationsflead.

Shapes diffuse and intertwine,
Reflections waver, redefine,
In the depths of the design,
Truths obscurely realign.

Now the mirror's image sway,
Tempering the light of day,
Journey's end, come what may,
Weaking frayed, yet still we stay.

Shards of Being

Crystals splitting in their flight,
Colours prismatic in their fight,
Refracting lives caught in the light,
Scattering selves, day and night.

Embers dance in shadowed glow,
Flickers of the past bestow,
Broken windows, ages show,
Fragmented stories others know.

Every crevice hides a tale,
Whispers on the winds prevail,
Voices rise, though frail, scale,
Across the void, beyond the veil.

Tapestries of time unfurl,
In the midst of storm, twirl,
Lost within the chaos, swirl,
Finding forms in this world.

Each shard a universe apart,
A mirror's soul, a beating heart,
Fragments joined, yet torn apart,
Crafting bonds none can thwart.

Scattered Truths

In windswept fields of shifting thought,
Truths once found, now often fought,
Hidden in the tales we're taught,
Meanings scattered and distraught.

Echoes of the lives we've led,
Words unspoken, left unsaid,
Emerging from the books we've read,
Lie in fragments by the bed.

Wishes lost and dreams regained,
Through laughter, tears faint stained,
Reality and myth maintained,
In the balance, truths are strained.

Between the lines of day and night,
Clarity may come to light,
Illuminated, truths take flight,
In their fleeting, fleeting might.

Gather pieces, one by one,
Reconstruct beneath the sun,
Scattered truths, undone,
Now whole again, we've begun.

Fragmented Spectrum

Colors blend and yet they break,
Morning's light and evening's wake,
In a spectrum, dreams we stake,
Fragmented hues our hearts remake.

Moments caught in prisms bright,
Memories of day to night,
Shadows fall, then take their flight,
Refracting paths to find what's right.

Raindrops fall with hues confined,
In their depths, we seek, we find,
Pieces of the grand design,
Weaving through the fragile mind.

Light and dark, they twist and turn,
Fires of the soul that burn,
From the past to what we yearn,
In these fragments, lessons learn.

With every vision, newfound blend,
Colors shift, but truths transcend,
Fragmented spectrum, paths extend,
A radiant journey without end.

Scarred Reflections

In mirrors cracked, I see a face,
A visage worn by time's embrace,
Lines that speak of stories old,
Treasures lost and secrets told.

Eyes that search for what is gone,
A past where innocence shone,
In the shards, a fractured view,
Of days once bright, now subdued.

Memories whisper in the night,
Echoes of a distant light,
Through the glass, the years unfold,
Tales of love and hearts consoled.

Hands that trace the jagged lines,
Feel the pulse of ancient rhymes,
In these scars, a life revealed,
Wounds that time has tried to heal.

Reflections scarred, yet still they gleam,
A mosaic of a haunting dream,
Pieces whole yet incomplete,
In their fragments, truths we meet.

Splintered Dreams

In the hush of midnight's veil,
Dreams emerge, both frail and pale,
Splintered thoughts of what could be,
Float like ash upon the sea.

Hope's bright spark, a fleeting flame,
Chases shadows without name,
Promises in whispers sighed,
By the winds of time denied.

Fragments of a shattered dawn,
Yearn for futures never drawn,
In the grasp of sleep they lie,
Silent, lost beneath the sky.

Weaving through the breaks and seams,
Dwell the ghosts of broken dreams,
Haunting shades from yesternight,
Veiled in sorrow, dimmed in light.

Splintered dreams that fade and blur,
In the heart, their echoes stir,
Whispers of what once was sung,
Songs of visions left unsung.

Mosaic of Illusion

In a dance of shifting light,
Patterns weave through day and night,
Fragments merge, a cryptic maze,
Illusions shaped in twilight's haze.

Colors blend, a seamless flow,
Magic spun in undertow,
Pieces scattered, yet they form,
A tapestry both wild and warm.

In each shard, a secret gleams,
Truths entwined in waking dreams,
Mystery in every twist,
Hidden realms by starlight kissed.

Glimmers of a life unseen,
Echoes of what might have been,
Mirrored in the fractured glass,
Shadows dance and softly pass.

Mosaic bright with tales untold,
Ancient riddles to unfold,
In each sliver, worlds unite,
Illusions born of purest light.

Mirage of Fragments

In the desert's endless span,
Mirages form, where dreams began,
Fragments of a life half-seen,
Shimmering in golden sheen.

Truths dissolved by sun and sand,
Histories lost to changing land,
Figures vague in heat's embrace,
Answers hidden, no trace.

Phantoms in the distance yearn,
For the past they cannot turn,
Footprints fade in waves of heat,
Memories in time's deceit.

Fragments dance in taunting light,
Drawing near, then out of sight,
Promises in glimmers cast,
Fade before our reach at last.

Mirages of lives once dreamed,
In the desert's silence gleamed,
In their truths and lies entwined,
Whispers of what we can't find.

Glimmering Fractures

In twilight's gentle sigh,
Where shadows start to play,
The stars begin to lie,
And dusk turns into day.

Through cracked and broken panes,
The moonlight filters through,
Revealing hidden veins,
Of gold in twilight's hue.

A symphony of night,
Soft whispers in the breeze,
Each fracture catching light,
A silhouette of trees.

Darkness gently weaves,
Through fissures old and deep,
A tapestry that leaves,
Dreams lingering in sleep.

Glimmering in despair,
The fractures start to heal,
As moonbeams in the air,
Turn fantasies to real.

Cascading Shards

Beneath the sky's embrace,
The shards begin to fall,
Their edges soft with grace,
A dance that's slow and small.

Each fragment takes its time,
In cascading descent,
Reflecting light in rhyme,
As if in deep lament.

The ground receives the tears,
From heavens far above,
Each shard a whisper hears,
A song of broken love.

Yet, in their tumbling flight,
There's hope within each shard,
A glint of morning light,
A beauty unmarred.

Cascading through the night,
The shards form rivers bright,
A harmony in sight,
Of fractured dreams in flight.

Mirrored Illusions

Reflections in the glass,
Of worlds that seem so near,
Yet in the shadows pass,
Eluding all that's clear.

Mirrors hold their secrets,
In depths of silver lies,
Where dreams and thoughts beget,
The truth in hidden skies.

An image soft and fleeting,
A phantom of the mind,
In mirrored halls repeating,
What reason fails to find.

Illusions dance and shimmer,
In prisms of the night,
Their edges growing dimmer,
As dawn approaches light.

In mirrored worlds we wander,
Through realms of light and shade,
Yet truths we seek or ponder,
In illusions may fade.

Splintered Reflections

In pools of broken glass,
Forlorn reflections lie,
Each splintered shard en masse,
A fragment of the sky.

The scattered light refracts,
Through prisms of the soul,
And splintered truth enacts,
A part of the whole.

Each piece a shattered dream,
Held in a moment's grace,
Yet more than what they seem,
In every line and trace.

A tale of loss and gain,
In glints of broken light,
Where shadows cleanse the pain,
Of fractured wrongs and rights.

Splintered mirrors tell,
In silent breaths of night,
The echoes of a well,
Of dreams beyond our sight.

Reflected Ruination

In mirrors deep, a sorrowed face
An echo lost in time's embrace
Glass shards that whisper past's disdain
Reflecting ruin, silent pain

A fractured soul, in fragments gleams
Each piece a story, haunted dreams
Within the pane, a world decayed
By shadows cast, hopes once obeyed

The silvered surface tells its tale
Where joy doth sink, and sorrow sail
In every crack, a whispered plea
For solace in the broken sea

Yet midst the shards, a light obscured
A glimmer faint, yet reassured
That ruin's grasp shall not confine
The spirit's strength, in dark, divine

And from the depths, rebirth shall rise
To mend the heart, forgive the lies
In mirrored ruin, strength anew
As dawn breaks through the night's cold dew

Shadowed Cracks

Upon the wall, in silent space
A shadowed crack, a mem'ry's grace
It winds through time, it weaves through lore
A tale that's hidden, to explore

In each dark line, a whispered moan
Of days gone past, of hearts unknown
In shadow's breath, the secrets rest
Of sorrows deep, of life's great quest

Beneath the paint, beneath the hue
A million stories, faded, true
The shadowed cracks, they intertwine
An unseen art, a whispered sign

And in those cracks, the light doth play
A dance of dawn, a silent sway
Where darkness yields, a truth unfolds
In whispered shadows, life beholds

For cracks do tell what words can't reach
In silence deep, they softly teach
That in the shadows, light will dawn
To heal the cracks that life has drawn

Glimmers of Disarray

In chaos dances, glimmers bright
A fractured dream, in disarray's night
Each star a shard, each ray a plea
For order's touch, for harmony

Through tangled paths, the light does weave
A golden thread in night's wide sleeve
Within the chaos, patterns hide
Of life's grand tale, of fate's great tide

In every swirl, a vision's flash
Of moments gone, of futures dashed
Yet in the storm, a spark persists
A steadfast gleam, in time's great twists

The disarray, a canvas pure
Where chaos breeds, where stars endure
In glimmers small, a song does play
Of hope's refrain in disarray

For every gust, for every storm
A silent strength, a heart reborn
In glimmers bright, we carve our way
Through shadowed night, to break of day

Fractured Perceptions

In broken glass, the world is seen
A thousand views, a fractured sheen
Each sliver shows a piece of whole
A glimpsed truth, a splintered soul

With angles bent, perceptions change
The known becomes the new, the strange
In every crack, a hidden scene
Of life refracted, view serene

Through shattered lens, a beauty's traced
In every fault, a grace embraced
For in the break, new visions lie
Of heaven's reach, of earth's reply

The fractured view, a dance of light
Where dark and bright in chorus fight
In every shard, a world is born
Of hope, of pain, of night, of morn

Embrace the fractures, let them guide
For through the cracks, the truth resides
In every break, new worlds find birth
In shattered glass, we glimpse the earth

Fragmented Clarity

In shards of thought, we find our way
In echoes clear, yet far apart
Moments fleeting, drift away
Whispered truths that touch the heart

Between the fractures, light breaks in
Illuminates what we can't see
Puzzle pieces, worn and thin
Seeking out what's meant to be

Fragments scatter through our minds
Lost in shadows, grasp for light
Every piece a tale it binds
Guiding us through darkest night

A mirrored world of shattered dreams
Reveals the paths we cannot tread
Through the storm, a fleeting gleam
Guides us where our fears have fled

In broken bits, the whole we find
A clarity beyond the glass
Through the chaos, forms align
Building bridges from the past

Splintered Gaze

Eyes that see through cracks in time
Reflections tremble, softly break
A splintered gaze, so pure, sublime
In fragments, dreams begin to wake

A world within a shattered lens
Truth and lies, their lines entwine
Broken views, yet they transcend
Emerging patterns, so divine

Through splinters, we can see anew
In pieces, light begins to bend
Every fracture holds a clue
To truths concealed beyond the end

Visions shaped by time and space
In splintered sight, the whole is found
Fragmented glimmers interlace
In brokenness, we are unbound

Splintered dreams within our sight
Reflections of a past unmade
In every shard, a spark of light
In fractured clarity, unafraid

Fractured Radiance

Radiant beams in fractured sprawl
Dancing light through dark's embrace
Shattered gleams where shadows fall
Illuminate the hidden space

The sun's warm touch in broken rays
Finds pathways through the jagged night
A fractured sky, a world of graze
Where splintered moments feel so right

In cracks, the luminescence weaves
A tapestry of golden threads
In every break, the darkness leaves
A whisper where the daylight spreads

Brilliant shards of light and dark
Puzzle pieces of the day
Fractured radiance leaves its mark
Guiding us along our way

Splintered beams of sun and shade
Create a world both bright and dim
In fractured rays, the fears that fade
Reveal the joy within the whim

Broken Perspectives

Through broken glass, the world distorts
Shapes and shadows, blend and shift
A view where every angle courts
A truth that can both wound and lift

In jagged frames, perspectives twist
Revealing what we too soon miss
A fractured view, a hidden tryst
A world that lies within a kiss

The cracks define, the light breaks through
Creating forms we can't explain
In brokenness, we find the new
A path through joy, a path through pain

Perspectives shattered, yet they bind
A deeper sense of what can be
In broken views, our souls aligned
A tapestry of mystery

Each fragment holds a universe
Of hopes and dreams, of fears concealed
In brokenness, we find the verse
Where all our truths are then revealed

Broken Echoes

In the hollow, whispers dwell,
Echoes dance, a mournful spell,
Memories fracture, dreams dispel,
In the quiet, secrets swell.

Silent phantoms, shadows play,
Fragments of a distant day,
Hope and sorrow, shades of gray,
Lingering whispers fade away.

Through the mist, the voices weep,
In the twilight, shadows creep,
Lost in time, where echoes seep,
In the dusk, the silence deep.

Forgotten tunes, the air is thin,
In the void, where sound begins,
Etched in darkness, etched within,
Echoes broken, lost to winds.

Fragmented Self-Portrait

Pieces scattered, who am I?
Splintered mirror, fractured sky,
In reflection, shadows vie,
Fragmented dreams, a silent cry.

Mosaic fragments, colors blur,
Faces merge, in whispers stir,
Lost in echoes, thoughts occur,
In the pieces, who we were.

Shards of memory, pieces fall,
Building walls, where shadows call,
Silent echoes, down the hall,
Fragments hold a hidden thrall.

In the glass, a fleeting face,
Broken time, a fractured space,
Silent whispers, leave no trace,
In the fragments, we embrace.

In the Shattered Light

Crimson beams of fractured dawn,
Through the shards, the day is drawn,
Symbols of a world withdrawn,
In the shattered light, we're gone.

Glimmering in the broken sun,
In the cracks, the shadows run,
Silent echoes long begun,
Shattered light where dreams are spun.

Illuminating phantoms play,
Through the shards, the colors stray,
Light refracting, night to day,
In the shards, where time will lay.

Embedded in the fractured glow,
Reflections where the spirits flow,
In the shattered light, we show,
What lies beyond, we may not know.

Crescendo of Shards

Sound of silence, broken screams,
In the whispering, broken dreams,
Shattered hopes in silent streams,
Where the endless echo teems.

Symphony of fractured thought,
Melodies of sorrow sought,
In the shards, the battles fought,
Where the broken silence taught.

Cries of triumph, whispers thin,
Echoes of where dreams begin,
In the fragments, screams within,
Harvesting the shards of sin.

Resonating through the pain,
Shattered notes of broken chain,
In the shards, we feel the strain,
Crescendo of the shattered reign.

Tangled Shards

In midnight's grasp, the shadows wind,
Within the silent, aching park,
Fragments of memories entwined,
Beneath the stars, the skies so dark.

Echoes whisper of time gone by,
As tangled shards lay 'cross the field,
Each glimmering tear, a mournful sigh,
A past that dreams would not yield.

From broken glass, reflections fall,
On paths that lead to nowhere clear,
A distant call, a haunting pall,
As twilight's end will soon appear.

The wind it breathes a song of old,
Through branches bare, and nights so cold,
The tangled shards of stories hold,
In dreams they silently unfold.

Kaleidoscopic Ruins

Through fractured beams in morning light,
Where shattered ceilings brightly gleam,
A world of colors lost in flight,
Kaleidoscopic ruins dream.

Each shard a tale, a broken hue,
In vivid chaos, beauty lies,
The crumbling stones of thoughts anew,
Through prisms of forgotten skies.

Once grand halls now kissed by vines,
Embrace the echoes faint and near,
The silent dance of shifting lines,
Paints memories with hues unclear.

From patterned glass and beams askew,
A dance of shadows does ensue,
Kaleidoscopic ruin's view,
Where past and present both construe.

Dissolved Views

In misty shrouds, the dawn awakes,
Soft echoes tremble on the breeze,
The vision's edge, a veil that breaks,
Through morning's tender, fleeting pleas.

The past is but a whisper clear,
Dissolved in time's impartial hands,
Views of yonder fading near,
As grains of sand through fingers strand.

In twilight's blush, the hours depart,
Beneath horizons soft and wide,
Silent whispers haunt the heart,
Where dreams and memories collide.

A canvas washed in gentle hues,
Where shadows paint their silent news,
Dissolved views in morning's muse,
Whisper truths we all must choose.

Splintered Realms

In lands where shadows dare to tread,
Where moonlight's touch on waters shiver,
Splintered realms of dreams are spread,
Their seamless whispers drift and quiver.

Each step along the fractured path,
Through mirrored forests, endless nights,
Reveals a world of aftermath,
In splintered realms of haunting sights.

The silent calls from pasts unseen,
Echo through the vales and streams,
A world of twilight in between,
Where reality with fantasy teams.

The splintered realms of thought and time,
Hold secrets that no heart can mime,
In dreams they silently chime,
A melody beyond sublime.

Reflections in Ruins

Amidst the broken stone, I tread
Where whispers of the past have fled
Echoes linger, shadows sway
In ruins, dreams decay

Time has etched its silent scar
Wounds that heal, yet never are
Ghostly echoes of the night
Dance in ruins, out of sight

Shattered hopes in fragments lie
Beneath a dusky, hollow sky
Memories, a silent tide
In ruins, secrets hide

In the dust of yesteryears
Lie the remnants of our fears
Once, a place where life had bloomed
Now, in ruins, dreams exhumed

Yet in ruins, truth remains
Burned into these ancient plains
In reflections cold and stark
Ruins hold a silent mark

Fragments of Illusion

Mirrors twist the fleeting gaze
Labyrinths of light and haze
In illusions, truth is spun
Woven threads by midday sun

Shattered dreams, a fleeting spark
Fading fast as visions dark
In the fragments, shadows play
Lost in dreams of yesterday

Glimmering in twilight's sheen
Wonders of what might have been
Fragments lost in time's embrace
Mirror lies we dare not face

Echoes of the silent muse
Whispers of the truths we choose
In illusions, lives we mold
Fragmented tales, left untold

Yet within this broken stream
Lies a trace of what we dream
In the shards of night's confusion
Rest the fragments of illusion

Broken Glass Dreams

In broken glass, our dreams reflect
Shattered hopes we can't perfect
Fragments pierce the silent night
Fading in the morning light

Chasing visions, fragile, too
Mirrored worlds we thought were true
In the shards of glass they gleam
Broken dreams, a phantom scheme

Scattered pieces, sharp and cold
Stories that remain untold
Amongst the ruins of our past
Dreams in broken glass are cast

Splinters of what might have been
Haunting us from deep within
In these fragile moments seen
Are the dreams that might have been

Yet in glass, a beauty gleams
Wounds and scars, and broken dreams
In reflections, whispers call
Dreams in broken glass will fall

Splintered Silhouettes

Silhouettes that haunt the mind
Fractured shapes in shadows find
Pieces of what used to be
Splintered tales of memory

Casting shadows on the floor
Figures lost, and nothing more
Splintered echoes in the night
Fading fast with morning light

Fragments of a distant song
Splintered lives where we belong
Shadows dance in shades of grey
Ghostly figures drift away

Memories that slip away
Splintered figures, come what may
In the dark, they twist and bend
Silhouettes that never mend

Yet within these broken forms
Lies the truth in silent storms
Splintered, scattered, lost regret
Haunting, fading silhouettes

Cracked Reality

In a world that's bent and broken,
Shards of truths lie scattered pale,
Dreams once whispered, now unspoken,
Wander through this fragile veil.

Time's a river, ever splintered,
Rippling echoes, shadows cast,
Moments frayed and gently wintered
Twist and turn within the vast.

Mirrors crack with silent laughter,
Placid faces tell no tales,
Life's a play that's ever after,
Haunted by the cracks and trails.

Voices rise in disarray,
Songs of yesterday now pause,
Through the cracks where lights portray,
Glints of hope, despite the flaws.

In the fractal of existence,
Pieces find their place at last,
Broken, yet with sheer persistence,
Beauty forms where shadows passed.

Echoes of Fracture

Whispers linger in the crevice,
Where the broken dreams reside,
Silent screams of lost ambitions,
Stir the tranquil, pierce the tide.

Fragments of a once whole being,
Scattered 'cross the empty days,
Echoes bounce in endless seeing,
Lost within the mirrored haze.

Phantom voices, silent crying,
In the night where shadows play,
Burning stars in darkness lying,
Casting glows of fractured way.

In the depths of silent suffering,
Glimmers of a hope unfold,
From the echoes gently buffering,
Stories of the shards retold.

Pieces shift and slowly gather,
Bringing form to fleeting pain,
In the echoes they shall tether,
Fragments find their peace again.

Disjointed Visions

Through the veils of time and thought,
Visions scattered, chaos spun,
Flights of dream and cryptic fought,
Merge beneath the hidden sun.

Tattered scenes of disremember,
In the silence bind their fate,
Pieces fall from bright September,
As the twilight consecrate.

Fragments paint a disjoint storyline,
Silent frames in shifting light,
In the gap where dreams entwine,
Ghostly whispers mark the night.

Images in disarray,
Dance among the shaded seams,
Start and stop in wild display,
Warp the threads of primal dreams.

Disjointed visions, yet alive,
Pieces knit the broken view,
Where the shadows softly thrive,
Truths emerge through chaos' hue.

Mirror Maze Breakdown

In the maze of mirrored faces,
Truths reflect in distorted lines,
Shadows chase in haunted places,
Echoes wrap the silent signs.

Walls of glass in endless bending,
Fragment thoughts and shifting gleam,
Lost in mazes, never ending,
Life becomes a fractured dream.

Every path a new illusion,
Every step a mirrored clone,
Truth and lie in sheer confusion,
Lost within the echoing stone.

Silent cries through mirrored sorrow,
Flickering lights in disarray,
Hope and dread of no tomorrow,
Guide the weary hearts that sway.

In the maze of mirrored breaking,
Through the cracks a light shall shine,
In the fragments, new hope waking,
Pieces join and intertwine.

Splattered Reflections

On mirrored ponds where lilies drift,
Shattered glass, a sudden rift.
Stars alight in fractured lines,
Dreams disperse in hidden signs.

Rippled shadows, pale and thin,
Waves of time where we begin.
Faces splinter, merge anew,
Splattered reflections, morning dew.

Skies once clear now bear the stain,
Of moonlight's sorrow, silent rain.
Echoes twist through veils unseen,
Night's embrace, forever keen.

Fragmented souls in night's embrace,
Fleeting glimpses, moments trace.
In shards of glass our truths arise,
Splattered reflections, countless skies.

Fractured Gleam

Through the prism, colors bloom,
Breaking dawn in twilight's room.
Glimmers dance on edges sharp,
Fractured gleam, a fleeting spark.

Rays of light through crystal fraught,
Fragments hold what time forgot.
Whispers carried on a breeze,
Fractured gleam through twilight's trees.

In the depths of night's embrace,
Shattered dreams in lucid space.
Gleams once whole now intertwine,
Fractured light within the mind.

Beneath the stars where shadows creep,
Glimmered moments, secrets keep.
In that fractured, gleaming sphere,
Tales of old and future near.

Splintered Horizons

Horizons split by dawn's first light,
Colors clash in radiant sight.
Mountains echo tales untold,
Splintered hopes in sunrise bold.

Oceans rise with whispered dreams,
Waves of time in fractured streams.
In the distance, shadows fall,
Splintered horizons, standing tall.

The twilight brings a golden hue,
Crimson skies in shades of blue.
Splintered days and nights conflate,
Horizons merge, a twist of fate.

Silent winds through canyons sweep,
Whispers held in shadows deep.
In the splintered light of dawn,
Horizons break, yet life goes on.

In the Land of Cracks

Beneath the soil where secrets sleep,
Cracks of time through ages seep.
Roots that twist in hidden ways,
In the land where shadows blaze.

Mountains rise with broken peaks,
Cannons carved by nature's streaks.
In the fissures, stories lie,
Whispers of the earth and sky.

Rivers flow through cracked domain,
Tracing paths of joy and pain.
Cities built on fractured ground,
In the land where dreams are found.

In the silence of the night,
Stars align in fractured light.
In the land of cracks we stand,
Bound by earth, united band.

Splintered Souls

Broken dreams in twilight fade,
Wandering spirits, softly jade,
Echoes whisper through the trees,
Mist and shadows, memories freeze.

Silent tears in shadows fall,
Hearts divided, standing tall,
Fragments lost in time's embrace,
Splintered souls, a hidden grace.

Nightfall's veil, a weary cry,
Fading stars in an empty sky,
Hope entwined in whispers low,
In the dark, their stories flow.

Whispered prayers in silent night,
Seeking solace, seeking light,
Winds that carry tales untold,
Splintered souls, forever bold.

In the dawn, a fleeting dream,
Silver threads of what had been,
Pieces found, yet never whole,
Bound together, splintered souls.

Fragmented Echoes

Through the hallways of the past,
Echoes drift and shadows cast,
Bits of laughter, cries of woe,
Fragmented echoes softly flow.

Shattered mirrors, broken time,
In the distance, memories chime,
Pieces scattered far and near,
Fragments of what we held dear.

In the quiet, whispers blend,
Echoes of what could not mend,
Stories lost in silent screams,
Fragments torn from fractured dreams.

Winds that carry haunting songs,
Echoes of where hearts belong,
Pieces drift in endless space,
Fragmented echoes, lost in grace.

In the dusk, the echoes wane,
Blending with the falling rain,
Memories in shadows lie,
Fragmented echoes, passed us by.

Glass Shard Lullabies

Hushed beneath the moon's soft glow,
Shards of glass in moonlight show,
Fragments of a shattered sky,
Sing their glass shard lullaby.

Beneath the stars, the silence weaves,
Crystalline, among the leaves,
Fragments tinged with silver hue,
Lullabies of glass and dew.

In the wind, a whispered song,
Echoes of what once was strong,
Memories in shards of glass,
Lullabies through ages pass.

Gentle night, with tender care,
Holds the shards of dreams so rare,
Sing the lullabies of old,
Glass shard tales in night's soft fold.

When the dawn begins to break,
Shards of glass in light awake,
Dreams reborn from shattered highs,
Sing their glass shard lullabies.

Dissolved Illusions

Fleeting shades of midday sun,
Illusions cast but fleeting spun,
Dreams dissolve in amber light,
Memories dance in fading sight.

Shadows blend with night's embrace,
Whispers lost in time and space,
Illusions fade in twilight's climb,
Dissolved within the sands of time.

Morning dew with light refracts,
Fragments of those past impacts,
Dreams that wane and softly part,
Illusions melted from the heart.

Sunset hues in gentle streams,
Carry whispers of old dreams,
Dissolved within the twilight's song,
Illusions where they once belong.

When the stars ignite the sky,
Illusions slowly bid goodbye,
Memories in soft repose,
Dissolved within the night's sweet prose.

Fractals of Broken Light

In the twilight's gentle fold,
Broken light begins to dance.
Fractals of a story told,
Through the prism of a glance.

Shattered suns in teardrop beads,
Paint the sky with hues untamed.
Luminescence bends and bleeds,
From a heart that's unafraid.

Shivering spectra intertwine,
Colors weave in silent fight.
Whispers of the past align,
With the shadows of the night.

Hope refracted, dreams igniting,
In the glow of fractured grace.
Every shard, a new horizon,
Every piece, a cosmic chase.

Glimmers in the woven still,
Echo verses softly bright.
In the silent night they thrill,
Fractals of the broken light.

Glass Dust Memories

Memories engraved in dust,
Shards of glass that time forgets.
Echoes of a long-lost trust,
In the flicker of regrets.

Dreams dispersed in fragile grains,
Crystal whispers of the past.
Through the heartache and the pains,
Shattered moments ever last.

Glimpses of a world once whole,
Reflect in particles of dust.
Wandering through the fractured soul,
Teaching hearts to brave and trust.

Pale and fragile remnants lie,
Tracing paths in shifting light.
In the fragments, shadows sigh,
Stories of a silent fight.

Hope lies dormant in the haze,
Glass dust holding bygone dreams.
From the wreckage, futures blaze,
Crafted from the silent screams.

Shards of Vision

In a vision's broken pane,
Shards of sight diverge and gleam.
Fragmented truths in steady rain,
Stitch a kaleidoscopic dream.

Scattered on a canvas clear,
Pictures pulse in vibrant hues.
Each reflection drawing near,
Tales of joy and hidden blues.

Through the aching, jagged glass,
Eyes survey a distant shore.
Every splinter forms a pass,
Into worlds that hearts explore.

Images that dance on air,
Shrouded secrets, soft and bright.
Every quiet glare a prayer,
In the architecture of the night.

Fragments known and yet unknown,
Merge to form a sacred choir.
In the shards, a tale is shown,
Light's refracted, pure desire.

Broken Reflections

Mirrors cracked and hearts revealed,
Broken reflections whisper plain.
Truths so long and deeply sealed,
Flow like teardrops in the rain.

Silent echoes in the frame,
Glimpse the shadows shy and thin.
Where the light once fiercely came,
Now its fragments fade within.

Lines and fractures scribe the tale,
Splitting life in bright array.
Candor in the shards unveil,
Silent songs of yesterday.

Pulling strands of mirrored past,
Woven dreams of fractured views.
Through the looking glass, at last,
Truth emerges in the hues.

In the cracks, new worlds we see,
Beauty in the broken seams.
Reflections now set free,
Float on whispers, soft as dreams.

9 789916 748862